CONTENTS

There is so much beauty in Christmas. And every year, when this season rolls around, my heart can't wait to take it all in again. The time with family and friends, the special photo cards I receive from across the miles, the homemade sugar cookies decorated by small hands. It all feels like home. And it's the coming-together of all these small experiences that make me feel especially connected and loved.

And in the midst of the celebration, each year I look forward to sitting again with the Christmas story and marveling with fresh eyes at the gift we received 2000 years ago, and every day since.

Our God, who once felt distant, has come near through Jesus. He has gifted us with his presence, he has made us righteous through his blood, so that we can sit at his feet, free of guilt and shame.

Once, we were separated from God. But, because of Christmas — because of Jesus — we have been brought near.

As we walk slowly through the Christmas story, we'll look at how God not only invites us to come near, but through Jesus' example, also teaches us how. Consider Mary; Jesus' radical nearness begins as a baby growing in a mother's womb, being nourished by her body and comforted by her arms. It doesn't get any more *near* than that.

God doesn't *need* us for his plans to be fulfilled, but he *wants* us. He wants us to have an intimate connection with him and so he engages the human experience to tell His profound love story. It's super messy, but that's really the only way we could identify. He uses humble (broken, young, old, barren, stinky, brainy) and available people to tell His story, to remind us that we're all invited.

This Advent we will be moved by the Christmas story as we consider each detail leading up to the birth of Jesus, but we will also look at his supreme example of nearness and how we can live this example out in our own lives.

Love came near 2000 years ago. Love comes near, still. Jesus' love reaches us from the tops of our heads, to the tips of our toes and to the deepest, innermost parts of our heart.

Together, let's celebrate His gift of nearness this Christmas. He is God with us. Our Immanuel.

ABOUT ADVENT

The roots of Advent go very deep. The word "Advent" comes from the Latin word *adventus*, which means "coming" or "visit." Advent has evolved over the years, but today is most noted as a season of preparation for Christmas and begins the fourth Sunday before Christmas Day.

Some people mark Advent by lighting candles or hanging wreaths. Many have seen or used the popular calendars with candy, while some people give gifts. And others do all of the above.

But, one thing I believe we can all agree on is that Christmas is not something we can celebrate in just one day. It deserves a closer look.

So, whether Advent is rooted deep in your personal traditions or it's just a simple reminder to slow down, it is my hope that this 25-day Bible study will enhance your celebration of Jesus' coming, this Christmas season.

December

1

Read Exodus 24:1-2
Write Hebrews 4:16

What are the three levels of access to God's presence defined in this Exodus passage? Who is given access at each level?

This division of access takes place while the Israelites are wandering in the wilderness and is alluding to the tabernacle, where priests (Levites) are the only ones allowed behind the curtain (into God's presence). If you've studied this portion of the Old Testament, then you know that God's presence was (and is) something to be revered. The laws that were set in place while Moses lead the Israelites from Egypt to the Promised Land, were specific and not to be taken lightly.

What are the specific instructions to Moses in verse 2?

While the people of Israel have no direct access to God, Moses has a direct line. Exodus 33:11 (NIV) says, *"The Lord would speak to Moses face to face, as one speaks to a friend."*

I want to start our time in the Christmas story by looking back, before we move ahead. There are two accounts of the Christmas story in the Bible, one in Matthew and one in Luke. Over the next several weeks, we will read them both. But, especially in Matthew's telling of the story, there is great attention given to the connection between the old and the new. In Christian theology, this is known as "typology;" where a person, event or statement in the Old Testament points to or is fulfilled by Jesus in the New Testament.

Matthew used a lot of Moses typology in his telling of Jesus' birth story. What are some ways you see Moses' life point to Jesus' life? (Read 1 Timothy 2:5)

Moses' life alludes to Jesus in many ways. And, then there's the Israelites. And the Israelites lives and all their feeble efforts to obey... well, they allude to us. *We* are the Israelites; once left knees knocking, uninvited, at the bottom of the hill, relying on the word of another to tell us what to do.

But, now, *because of Jesus*, we are invited to come near.

Read Ephesians 2:13

Because Jesus left his seat at the right hand of God the Father and came to earth, atoned for our sins by his blood and made us holy, we can come directly to his throne. Into his presence boldly and confidently.

Because of Jesus, it's no longer Moses alone who can stand in the presence of God.

A God that once felt untouchable, has now become *"flesh and blood and moved into the neighborhood"* (John 1:14)(MSG).

Jesus, our Immanuel. God *with* us.

While the temple curtain won't be torn (a symbol of our direct access to God) until his death, Jesus' display of nearness begins the moment he left heaven and entered a mother's womb. It doesn't get any more *near* than that.

LOVE COMES NEAR

This is perhaps one of the most beautiful parts of the Christmas story and the reason we'll spend time each day this Advent to consider it. Jesus could have come to us in so many ways. He could have simply appeared supernaturally on the scene. But, he used us. He used Mary's womb and Joseph's humility. He partnered with John to spread the word, and gave spotlight to Elizabeth. He worked through the bonds of human love and friendship. He became like us, in every way, including a messy and naked arrival, vulnerable in the arms of a mother. He did this to be near us, but also, to *model* nearness *for* us.

So now, his radical invitation for nearness is also a radical *display* of nearness.

He doesn't just invite us to it. He shows us how it's done.

This Advent, I pray we come near to Jesus and feel overwhelmed by his nearness to us. I pray as we look deeply and intentionally at the Christmas story, we learn by Christ's example, how to better draw near to others and to him.

Hebrews 4:16 Let us then approach
God's throne of Grace with
confidence, so that we may receive
mercy + find grace to help us
in our time of need.

Isaiah 9:6
 For unto us a child is born
A son is given to us. And the
government is upon his shoulder;
And his name will be called
Wonderful Counselor, Mighty God,
Eternal Father, Prince of Peace.

Read Isaiah 9:2-7
Write Isaiah 9:6

Make a list of everything you see in this prophecy that points to the Messiah, Jesus.

There is perhaps no prophet in the Bible who points to the coming Messiah more than Isaiah. It's fascinating to look back at these passages and consider what God was doing when he spoke these words through the prophets hundreds and hundreds of years before they were fulfilled.

Read 2 Peter 1:19-21

What confidence does this passage give you about the prophecies given in the Bible? *Bible is complete truth!*

What does it mean that the prophets were "carried along by the Holy Spirit?" (v. 21) *The ideas & message were from God*

Read 1 Peter 1:10-12

Why is it important to know that the prophets had nothing to gain? (They were "serving not themselves but you"(v.12))
This is God's plan!

LOVE COMES NEAR

One point that stands out in this prophecy is right at the beginning. In verse 2 it says, "The people who walked in darkness have seen a great light..."

This alludes to the Christmas story as you consider the star that lead the Wise Men to Jesus. But, also to Jesus' power to bring the lost (those in darkness), to His light.

It gets personal when you consider that while this prophecy was partially fulfilled when Jesus came, it won't be completely fulfilled until Jesus returns. *Yes!*

Meaning, this prophecy is continually being fulfilled in us as co-laborers with Christ. We work to bring our friends, co-workers, neighbors and families into His light.

The peace of which "there will be no end" (v. 7) can't be found in darkness. Our world is in darkness. Many of those we love are in darkness. This prophecy of peace is realized today when new believers cross over from darkness to Light.

Who is God calling you to point to His light this Christmas? *Be BOLD*

December

3

A stump. The remains of a once strong, vibrant and life-filled tree, is now cut down. In the previous chapter of Isaiah, the prophet is telling about the once "lofty" Israelites, being cut down with an axe. *Disciplined.* The consequences of selfish, disobedient and arrogant choices.

After such a long cycle of obedience, followed by rebellion against God, it starts to feel like there's no hope for God's chosen people. And, then, out of the assumed-dead stump, life springs forth.

Consider drawing a picture of the stump of Jesse, based on Isaiah 11:1.

Describe how this image stirs hope in you. Nothing is to far gone for God to revive

What other visual images stand out to you from this passage? Consider drawing another illustration to represent them or simply write down the phrases that are most meaningful to you.

LOVE COMES NEAR

In what situation do you find yourself cut down this Christmas season? As we begin this time of waiting on Jesus, what specific places could you ask him for a fresh glimmer of hope? A tiny shoot of new life?

Read Romans 15:13

The same key ingredients that mark the origins of hope in this verse, are also key ingredients in the Christmas story: joy and peace. Because He came, they can be ours. There's always hope.

What are some specific ways you can pursue renewed hope in these areas that seem hopeless? Ask God to give you joy and peace, so that you may abound in hope by the Holy Spirit.

God, keep me centered on you + the joy + peace that you want me to feel.

My fave sentence: There's always hope!

Isaiah 11:2
The life giving spirit of God
will hover over him, the Spirit
that brings wisdom & understanding
The Spirit that gives direction &
builds strength.

Read Jeremiah 33:14-18
Write Jeremiah 33:16

Have you ever been stuck at the airport? You're on your way home from a long trip, your flight has been delayed and you have no way of getting home? And home is all you can think about? *There's no place like home*

This is a small taste of how the Israelite's felt. They have been driven from the Promised Land. They are stuck in a foreign land and have suffered many hardships. All they want is to go home. They haven't heard from God in years and they are losing hope.

This prophecy from Jeremiah states boldly that God will keep his promise. While the Israelites and even Jeremiah, have no clear way of knowing how this prophecy will be fulfilled, these words whisper hope to a desperate people.

Recall a time when you lost hope and God whispered his truth or his promises to you through a scripture? Write the scripture. *For I know the plans I have for you...*

Look through this passage and record any words and phrases you see that point to the true Messiah.

LOVE COMES NEAR

Verse 16 says, "And this is the name by which it will be called: '*The Lord is our righteousness*.'" The prophecy is saying that this town is going to look so radically different, they're going to change its name.

One beautiful detail about this passage, is when you look back at a nearly identical passage in Jeremiah 23:6, you'll see that the new ruler, the promised Messiah, is given the same name; "*The Lord is our righteousness*."

In the first reference we learn that as the prophecy is fulfilled, it's not the city that gets a new name, it's the people of God. *It's us.* And when we compare the first and second reference, we see how this prophecy points to our sharing in the name of Jesus.

Read 2 Corinthians 5:21

Because Jesus came and took our sin upon himself, as if it were his own, and took the punishment that we deserve, we are able to share in the righteousness of Christ.

Journal what it means to you to be in right standing with God, because of Jesus.

Jeremiah 33:16

In those days Judah will be saved & Jerusalem will live in safety. This is the name by which it will be called: The Lord our Righteous savior

Read Hebrews 7:11-19
Write Hebrews 7:18-19

This passage has a lot of layers. There are a lot of different dots to connect, to pull out all its rich truths. So, here are a few key details to help you put the pieces together.

1. Melchizedek was noted for being both a king and a "priest of God Most High" (Gen 14:18-20).

2. Christian Jews were struggling with returning to their normal ways of Judaism after Jesus and trying to wrap their heads around how their old sacrifices didn't work anymore. They were the original recipients of this message.

It's a lot of detail, but write a summary of verses 11 - 14.

In the Old Testament, the Jewish person's only chance to be made pure was through the law. But, it was hopeless. This passage was written to help Jewish Christians accept and understand how the traditions of the Levitical priesthood and the Mosaic Law, were no longer necessary.

Note the power source in verse 16. Write a summary for verses 15-19.

LOVE COMES NEAR

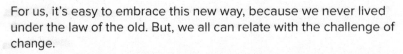

No more sacrifices? No more ceremonies? Yes, please.

For us, it's easy to embrace this new way, because we never lived under the law of the old. But, we all can relate with the challenge of change.

What qualities emphasized in verse 19 about this "new hope" do you think were most meaningful to Jewish Christians? What qualities are most meaningful to you?

No longer separated by imperfect rules, near impossible to perform. Our hope is now secure, in the warm embrace of our Father.

Hebrews 7:18-19 NIV
The former regulation is set aside because it was weak + useless (for the law made nothing perfect), + a better hope is introduced, by which we draw near to God

Better Hope! → JESUS!

Read Matthew 1:1-16
Write John 15:16

A list like this in the Bible is easy to gloss over. But, this list is worth a slow read. I encourage you to pick one, two or more of the following passages to get a picture of the people who make up Jesus' genealogy.

It's a pretty colorful group of people. And a great reminder of God's ability to redeem and to choose anyone for his purpose.

Choose one or more of the following passages to read:

Judah, the father of Perez and Zerah by Tamar// Read Genesis 38
Rahab // Read Joshua 2
Uriah's wife // 2 Samuel 11

Journal your reaction to this cast of characters chosen as Jesus' ancestors. *Sinners! Unlikely but perfect examples of what God can credeem & use!*

LOVE COMES NEAR

Fill in your family tree (on page 17).

What traits from each grandparent do you want to remain in your family history? What traits do you want to leave in the past?

What traits from each parent do you want to remain? What traits would be better left in the past?

Consider the verse we wrote out today; John 15:16. **How does the truth of this verse encourage you?**

God uses us in spite of us. He chooses us, knowing full well our brokenness.

Pray over your list of good and bad traits. Ask God to give you wisdom to sow healthy emotional seeds into your family, and receive his grace for the broken places. Thank God that an invitation into His story doesn't require that we have it all together.

Linda Susan
Your Name

Cynthia Irish
Mom

Richard Hockins
Dad

Ralph O. Irish
Madje Samson
Maternal
Grandparents

Stanley Martin Hockins
Lillian Krieps
Paternal
Grandparents

John 15:16
You did not choose me, but I chose you & appointed you so that you might go & bear fruit - fruit that will last - and so that whatever you ask in my name the Father will give you.

Read Luke 1:5-17
Write Luke 1:13

What details about Zechariah and Elizabeth are given in verses 5-7?

Barrenness carried a painful stigma in this society. It was assumed that someone must have really upset God. But, the scripture points out that both Zechariah and Elizabeth were blameless.

What does this detail of blamelessness say to you about God's sovereignty in their lives?

There were likely about 20,000 priests during this time. They were divided into 24 groups and each group was called up to serve at the temple only twice each year. With thousands of priests in each group, it was likely that serving at the temple was a once-in-a-lifetime opportunity for Zechariah. But, we know that the timing of this and his being chosen "by lot" was no mistake.

What instructions and information does the angel give to Zechariah about his son? (Note the prophecy fulfilled from Malachi 4:6)

Zechariah and Elizabeth are an amazing example of faithfulness. While other priests were into making a show of their religious status, they showed their faith "*before God*." Meaning, it wasn't necessarily in plain view of man. While other men would have divorced their wives because of barrenness, Zechariah was devoted to his wife. I picture them an aged couple, who against all odds, have made a happy, content life together.

Who do you know who models faithfulness, against all odds?

LOVE COMES NEAR

When we look closely at the details given about John in this passage, two things stand out: the obvious detail is that John is set apart and the second is that John's purpose is to bring delight to his parents.

Love comes near in this scenario when God answers the longing of two parents' hearts, by giving them a son. Any couple who has longed for a family, and then been given the joy of a child, can relate to this elation.

The angel says, this boy will bring great amounts of "joy and gladness," for his parents and for many others. While the key details of the angel's announcement are of John set apart for God's work, the angel doesn't neglect to tell how this baby is a hand-delivered, straight up gift from the Father, meant to bring great joy to these faithful parents. God has heard the cries of two longing hearts. And he answered.

What gifts can you reflect on that have brought you great joy?
Read Matthew 7:11 and James 1:17
Take a moment to give thanks to God for the gifts in your life.

Read Luke 1:18-25
Write John 1:16

No one ever said Zechariah was perfect. Just faithful.

What answer does the angel give to Zechariah's questioning?

God should have struck him dead or revoked the announcement. There stands Zechariah, in the temple, in the presence of God, and an angel appears before him. Yet, his faith still wavers.

Whether because of doubt, discouragement or delay, in what areas do you lack faith that God will answer your prayers?

At the end of this passage, we learn that Elizabeth remains secluded for the first five months of her pregnancy. **Why do you think she did this?**

Sometimes, we rush to friends and family to share good news, or to share in sorrows, and neglect rushing to our knees. For whatever reasons Elizabeth kept her pregnancy quiet, we can appreciate her example of making worship a priority during the greatest surprise and joy of her life.

LOVE COMES NEAR

We serve a God who gives multiple chances. Getting it right the first time isn't always required.

Zechariah was faithful, but like you and me, he was human. His punishment for his faltering faith at a critical moment was a rebuke from God, but it was a gracious rebuke.

I'd say every rebuke from God could be categorized as gracious, but can you recall a particularly gracious rebuke in your life? How did it influence your walk with God?

How do you imagine God used this season of silence in Zechariah's life?

Read Proverbs 3:11-12 and Hebrews 12:11

How do discipline and love go hand in hand?

Read Luke 1:26-38
Write Luke 1:37

What stands out to you about Mary's reaction?

List all the promises made about the Messiah in this passage.

Mary then has a question, though it's not filled with doubt, as we saw with Zechariah, but expectation. "*How will this be...?*" Her question is more inquisitive than uncertain. She believes and she's curious to know the details, given the intimate nature of the situation.

The angel announces that the child will be called "holy", the son of God. Because he is not born of a man, he won't inherit the same sinful nature that the rest of us received. He is truly set apart.

To strengthen her faith even more, the angel tells her about Elizabeth.

How does verse 37 stir your heart?

What can we learn from Mary in her humble submission to this assignment?

LOVE COMES NEAR

God gives us grace for the journey. And often he does it in the form of friendship. Our relational God knew that Mary would likely need support, but with a story as far-fetched as hers, not many, if any, would understand or even believe her. Then I imagine the angel said, "*I already thought of that.*"

He tells her about Elizabeth, to immediately strengthen her faith in God and to remind her she is not alone and that "*nothing is impossible*" when God is in the mix.

Recall a time when God used a friend to strengthen your faith.

Read Hebrews 10:24-25

How does this verse and Mary and Elizabeth's example encourage your heart towards community?

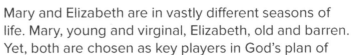

Read Luke 1:39-45
Write Luke 1:45

Mary and Elizabeth are in vastly different seasons of life. Mary, young and virginal, Elizabeth, old and barren. Yet, both are chosen as key players in God's plan of salvation for the world. Not because of anything they had done to earn or deserve it, but simply because they were faithful and they chose to believe God's promise.

Why did Mary go with "haste" to visit Elizabeth?

It would be easy to assume Mary's "greeting" to Elizabeth was a quick, bursting through the door with a hug and a "Hello!", type of event. But a traditional greeting during this time would have likely included a lengthy exchange of details and updates from their lives. This is where Mary shares the events of the angel visiting her, and Elizabeth responds, "No way! Me too!" *Or so I imagine.*

What words and emotions do you suppose were exchanged during this greeting? *It must have been comforting*

What do we learn about the faith of Mary and Elizabeth?

LOVE COMES NEAR

There are many stories in the Bible, when men or women of faith were asked to do bold, scary, things in His name. And when they asked for God to show them a sign that it was really Him leading them, he often did it. (Read Judges 6:36-40 for one example) *Gideon - fleece*

God knows that sometimes we need assurance. That our emotions can get the best of us and quickly cloud the truth. When God says, "Go", we should simply go! He is worthy of our going at his word. But, in his grace towards us, he knows sometimes we need a little more.

Mary and Elizabeth were living in a time when there hadn't been much prophesying. They hadn't seen any miracles. Their faith was built on the promises of truths passed down to them from generations before.

Sometimes, when the calling is big, we need big affirmation and encouragement to go along with it. And when we ask, God is gracious to provide it.

Recall some ways God has affirmed your calling. *Conversations Music Messages*

How has God used you to affirm and encourage your brothers and sisters in Christ?
I pray that he has! Devotions

Luke 1:45

Blessed is she who believed that the Lord would fulfill his promises to her!

December

11

Mary may be young. But, she gets it. In this passage, called "Mary's Song" or "The Magnificat", her overwhelming joy and her profound praise are evidence that God knew what he was doing when he chose this girl.

"Mary's Song" begins with thankfulness. List all the ways Mary gives thanks in verses 46-49.

The second part of her song talks about what her son's birth will mean for believing Israelites.

List the blessings Mary states Jesus' birth will bring in verses 50-55.

LOVE COMES NEAR

God chooses unlikely people. Unlikely, but available. Mary and Elizabeth are wonderful examples of this in the Christmas story. Both of the women also exhibit great humility.

Elizabeth says, "*And why is this granted to me that the mother of my Lord should come to me?*" (Luke 1:43). Mary says, "*... he has looked on the humble estate of his servant ...*" (v.48)

As Mary senses His nearness, her heart is overwhelmed with joy. She has no ego to crowd out her magnificent God.

Read Proverbs 29:23 and James 4:10

We make room for God, when we get out of the way.

In what ways are you proud? How can you get out of the way and how might God use you if you did? What joy might you experience?

When we make much of our lives, of our own accomplishments, we cannot fully grasp the greatness of our God or experience the fullness of his joy.

Read Matthew 1:18-21
Write Matthew 1:21

After spending three months with Elizabeth, it's time for Mary to return home. I can't imagine all the emotion that Mary is feeling, facing her friends and family, and Joseph. And I can't imagine all that Joseph was feeling, being torn between her story and what seemed like opposing evidence.

List the range of emotion that both Mary and Joseph must have felt during this time.

What does Joseph's decision in the matter say about his character and his feelings for Mary?

List all the promises made about the Messiah in the angel's proclamation.

"*You shall call his name Jesus, for he will save his people from their sins.*" (v.21) It was common for people to name their sons Jesus. It was a symbol of hope for those who hoped in the prophesied Messiah. A hope that a savior would come and rescue them from oppression. But, the angel points out his grander purpose. Jesus will come, not simply to save the Israelites from oppression, but to save the whole world from their sins.

LOVE COMES NEAR

Do you notice how the angel addressed Joseph? "*Joseph, Son of David.*" The angel calls him by name, tells him not to be afraid and then, reminds him of his heritage. *Oh, that's powerful.* Joseph is a member of the family line of David. The family line of which the prophecies told would bring forth the Messiah. With that one sentence, Joseph goes from clouded confusion to clarity. His purpose is clear.

I'm sure Joseph knew the prophecies. Perhaps humility had kept him from considering it before, or just the fact that it had been so long since the prophecies were spoken, but here is the angel with the proclamation:

It's you, Joseph. I'm going to use you to help fulfill this promise.

At just the right time, love comes near and gives us a pep talk. It takes us out of the lies and points us to what's true.

In what ways do you feel inadequate for the task?

Read Isaiah 43:1

Remember whose *you are.*

Read Matthew 1:22-25
Write Matthew 1:23

In Matthew's telling of the birth story of Jesus, he is adamant about pointing to the birth of Jesus as specific fulfillment of Old Testament prophecy. There are five different times in Matthew, where he says something like what we see in verse 22: "*All this took place to fulfill...*"

Read Isaiah 7:14

When these words were originally uttered hundreds of years earlier, it would have been impossible to predict that God would fulfill them as he did. And Matthew's mission is to show the unity of God's plan, by emphasizing the unity between the Old Testament and the New.

What additional detail does Matthew give in verse 23, that's missing from Isaiah 7:14?

Why do you think Matthew is sure to mention this detail?

What does Joseph do after he wakes up from his encounter with the angel? Write down the specific ways Joseph was obedient.

LOVE COMES NEAR

I think it's important to remember that God has always been Immanuel. He has always been with us. This title for God is used in the Old Testament. It's a name for God's sovereign intervention and defense of his people. But, in Jesus (especially with Matthew's emphasis in verse 23) our eyes are open to its new depth in meaning. Yes, he's with us. But, now he's *with* us. He's here, with skin on, breathing the same air, in and out.

While the name "Jesus" (our Savior) points to what he will do (save us), the name "Immanuel" points to who he is. He is God *with us*. And when you hear his name this Christmas, when you sing "O Come Immanuel" in your caroling or Sunday worship, I pray you are renewed in your awe of it. I pray your heart explodes with thankfulness over this new layer of nearness we have received by his arrival on earth.

How do you see these two distinct aspects of Immanuel today? In what ways do you see his sovereignty in your life and in the world? In what ways do you feel him close to you, like he's a guest at your dinner table?

14

This passage is a beautiful foreshadowing of the Messiah. Because the Israelites are under affliction, this announcement of a great ruler gives them great hope.

Christmas is a celebration of the shadows, whispers and hopes of us all, becoming a reality.

What hints toward the Messiah jump out at you from this passage?

Here are a few not to be missed:

"But you, O Bethlehem ... who are too little..."
Even from the whispers of Jesus hundreds of years before his arrival, we see him using unexpected vessels to tell his story.

"...whose coming forth is from of old, from ancient days."
The Israelites assumed this meant from the line of David, and they were right. But, they didn't know the deeper truth, that while the Messiah was to be *born* in Bethlehem; Bethlehem is not where he *began*. A great part of the gift of His coming, is remembering he willingly left his seat in heaven to be with us. And, that God's plan of the ages has always included Jesus. **Read Ephesians 1:4 and 1 Peter 1:20.**

"And he shall stand and shepherd his flock..."
Shepherding is a dirty job. Not a career that many aspired toward. But, it's an accurate picture of what Jesus does for us and scripture uses this parallel often. This prophecy hints at the shepherd's involvement in the Christmas story. His use of shepherds as the first witnesses of Jesus' birth, it's another example of God using humble people as his vessels.

"... for now he shall be great to the ends of the earth..."
Alluding to a Savior for all mankind, both Jew and Gentile.

LOVE COMES NEAR

Another hint in this prophecy is the final line that says, *"And he shall be their peace."*

I imagine the Israelites read this line and assumed it meant that he would bring them peace among their enemies. But, he doesn't intend to simply bring peace. He will *be* peace.

Read Ephesians 2:14

The peace that Jesus became, is not a conditional peace. Or a temporary peace. It's a supernatural peace that we can access, once we accept His gift of salvation.

Read Psalm 34:14

Just like all God's gifts, they are ours for the taking. But, sometimes we aren't willing to do the work. To make the changes necessary to walk in God's peace.

In what ways do you need peace this Christmas? How can you actively pursue His peace?

Read Luke 2:1-7
Write Luke 2:7

"But you, O Bethlehem, who are too little to be among the clans of Judah..."

We've read the prophecy in Micah. But, Mary and Joseph are in Nazareth. So, how will the prophecy be fulfilled? *Enter God.* The great orchestrator of details, both big and small.

He puts it on the minds of government officials to require a census, of course. A detail that affects the entire Roman world, for the purpose of one husband and wife, precisely at the time their baby would be born.

Read Proverbs 21:1

Even when our world *feels* out of control, it's not. God is in the details, and there's not one that gets past him. Whether it's world leaders, politicians, evil extremists, drought, earthquakes, disaster or disease. He reigns supreme.

How does this build your confidence in God's power?

Mary and Joseph will go to Bethlehem to fulfill the prophecy, but it would seem that the logistical details were less than ideal for them, especially for Mary. This call to "Go" requires Mary, nine months pregnant, to travel to a city on top of a mountain via donkey, and give birth in a barn.

We know God has the power to make these circumstances more appealing. **After God influences an empire for his purposes, why do you think he chose to leave them without a room in the inn?**

LOVE COMES NEAR

Sometimes we glamourize the Christmas story. We see Mary in the nativity, hair and dress intact, and we think, "How clean and nice." And it makes us feel warm and toasty inside.

We can easily get disillusioned about the reality of her situation.

I consider a couple in my church who will soon pack up their two small children and move to Haiti to serve as missionaries. From the outside, we can marvel at their decision and think about how pleased God must be with their obedience. All true and good. But, in the nitty gritty daily grind, they're working hard to figure out all the details of uprooting their lives, of raising financial support, of homeschooling their children, and saying goodbye to the comforts of the home they know and the comforts of nearby family.

When has your calling lead you into not so ideal circumstances? How was God working in you through that situation? What would you want the world to know about God's work in you during that time?

God is always more concerned with our character, than our comfort. It's why sometimes, he calls us to the messy and the hard things. The things that stretch our security and make our stomach do flip-flops. I'm sure it's why he did it in Mary's life, too.

Read Isaiah 48:10

What do you think Mary would say to us today about saying "yes" to the hard things?

Read Luke 2:8-12
Write Luke 2:10

Unsuspecting. Unassuming. Undeserving. A group of shepherds witness the angel's display. An unlikely audience, but not an accidental one.

Imagine how it must have felt to be the shepherds. As a profession, shepherding wasn't given much value. Shepherds weren't used to receiving special attention. They must have assumed a visitation like this was some kind of mistake. Surely it was meant for someone else.

Read 1 Corinthians 1:26-31

Based on the truth of this passage, why did God choose the shepherds to make His great announcement?

There seems to be a theme in those through whom God chose to tell the Christmas story: humility. There was no ego in the way for the shepherds. All the glory went to God.

"*I bring you good news...*" The angels have good news, and the good news is here. "Good news" is translated "gospel." The Gospel message. The Truth is here.

According to Luke 2:10, who is the Good News for?

The prophecies pointed to this, and the angels make it official. Good news of great joy, indeed.

LOVE COMES NEAR

Perhaps you've seen the trend amongst the appearance of angels in the Christmas story? We see it with Zechariah, Joseph, Mary and now the shepherds.

With each encounter, the angel's message begins with assurance. "*Fear not...*"

The message the angels brought was profound. It was a message for all of us; but in the moment, a message that was deeply personal to each recipient. To each, it was a call to something radical, that would require great faith and more than a few challenges.

Fear is our natural human response to a call to do hard things. But, the angel knows this. God knows this.

Love comes near in the Christmas story, as God addresses our human weaknesses, before he calls us to action.

Read Psalm 118:6 and Isaiah 41:10

We tend to get scared about the same stuff again and again. **In what ways do you battle fear in your life?**

When Jesus came, he defeated death. What's scarier than dying? Because death is defeated, we are liberated. Armed with God's promises and his tender assurance, we can kick fear in the teeth and boldly do hard things in the name of Jesus.

God has kingdom work for each of us to do. And fear would love to get in the way of it. **What kingdom work might you pursue without hesitation, if fear were out of the picture?**

This Advent, anytime you see an angel, whether it be on a Christmas card or on top of a tree, let it serve as a reminder of God's great promise and his tender assurance, that we have nothing to fear.

Read Luke 2:13-18
Write Luke 2:14

The angels are bursting at the seams, in praise of God. Thousands of them, singing together this message of glory to God and peace to mankind. Can you imagine the drama of this moment?

I love that God holds nothing back in announcing the birth of his Son. A proud Daddy.

What words would you use to describe the angel's announcement?

What action did the shepherds take after the angels left the scene?

LOVE COMES NEAR

So the shepherds told a few locals about the event. But, it didn't start an uproar in Bethlehem.

The angel's visit wasn't about the shepherds. And it wasn't about starting some large scale campaign. It was about the praise God deserved. While earth didn't yet know what hit them, the heavens erupt in praise. *Heaven knows.*

I love the contrast between what is happening on earth and what's happening in heaven. On earth, his entry is humble in every way you can imagine. But, heaven cannot contain its excitement.

Have you ever been witness of something profound from God? A miracle or a clearly divine affirmation of His goodness?

How did you see God's purposes fulfilled in what you experienced? How did you/can you give God the glory for what you witnessed?

When God shows up, and we stand as witnesses, it's never a celebration of our worth, but His.

Read Luke 2:19-21
Write Luke 2:19

How would you describe the reactions of both Mary and the shepherds?

Circumcision on the eighth day after birth was commanded under Mosaic Law (Genesis 17:12-14).

LOVE COMES NEAR

Our lives move at a fast pace. I don't know who made those rules, but, somehow we follow them. We pack our schedules to the max, leaving little room for extras.

The Christmas season is no exception. And may, in fact, be the rule.

This Advent, let's take a cue from Mary and take time to ponder God.

Read Psalm 4:4, 77:12 and 143:5

Take five minutes today and ponder God. Meditate on Him. Close your Bible and put down your pen. Ponder scripture and search your heart. Celebrate that because Jesus came, we have direct access to the Father. You can pour out your heart to him without hesitation.

If this is a new practice for you, consider trying the palms down, palms up exercise. I first learned about it while reading "Celebration of Discipline" by Richard Foster. You begin by placing your palms down. This symbolizes your desire to turn over your concerns to God. Tell God what's on your heart and release it to him. After you've expressed all your anxious places and cares, turn your palms up. This represents your desire to receive from the Lord. Ask God for the help you need regarding these concerns. Then, spend a few minutes in silence, simply enjoying His presence.

God-honoring meditation is a valuable spiritual discipline. One that can be hard to prioritize. When our culture wants us to rush through this season, determine that this Advent, you will take time to slow down. Anticipate his coming and offer him the praise and adoration he deserves.

Luke 2:19 But Mary treasured
up all these things and
pondered them in her heart

Read Matthew 2:1-2
Write Isaiah 60:3

What is most surprising to you in these two verses in Matthew?

For being "wise" men, it seems unwise to me that they would go to the current king of the Jews (Herod), a man with a hot temper and a huge ego, and ask for his help to find the baby who would one day usurp his throne, so they could worship him. But, maybe the mistake is only that obvious in hindsight. I think they must have assumed that since Herod was himself Jewish, that he was already aware of the new king, or that the new king was, in fact, Herod's child.

Regardless, God uses these unlikely characters to tell his story.

What Godly purpose do you see for including the Wise Men and Herod in the Christmas story?

Reread Isaiah 60:3 and read Numbers 24:17

The Jews believed these Old Testament prophecies pointed to a messianic deliverer.

Write any thoughts or reflections you have about seeing the fulfillment of these prophecies in Jesus' birth story.

LOVE COMES NEAR

The "east" had a reputation for wisdom. **Read 1 Kings 4:30**. God made Solomon wiser than the people out east. *That was a big deal.* The Wise Men in our story were likely very smart, and were also likely into astrology. They studied the stars and were probably fascinated by them. So, because of their extensive study, they would have been wise in the ways of many cultures, and keyed in on the prophecies of scripture that referenced stars or bright lights.

So, how intimate and how wise that God would draw the Wise Men to Jesus in a way that made sense to them. We don't know how the story ends for the Wise Men after their encounter with Jesus, but I love this glimpse of how it began.

How has God drawn you to himself in unique and special ways? What or whom did he use to first point you to Jesus?

December 20

Bullies are good at appearances. They bark and puff up their chests. They use big words and shake their fists. But, peak behind the curtain and you'll find fear, anger, insecurity... a big and scary front door, sitting on a crumbling foundation.

Israel's corrupt religious and political leadership has been threatened. Herod's throne is threatened. The rumor is spreading throughout Jerusalem that the hundreds year old prophecy of the Messiah might be coming true. And everyone's nervous.

What does the fact that Herod himself didn't know the scriptures about the Messiah tell you about Israel's leadership at the time?

This is the beginning of a groundswell in the story of Jesus. God is rattling the cages of a giant who has enjoyed a long nap in the lap of luxury.

How would you describe Herod's approach in dealing with the Wise Men? How is this characteristic of his leadership and of Israel at the time?

LOVE COMES NEAR

The other characters in this passage were the chief priests and the scribes. The religious leaders of the time. They hear the Wise Men's story and they recall for Herod the prophecy. And then, what do they do? *Absolutely nothing.*

Is that surprising to you? Shouldn't the religious leaders, the ones who've spent their lives studying, teaching and interpreting the scriptures, be moved by the Wise Men's announcement?

What reasons can you assume for why the religious leaders didn't react?

Read Matthew 15:7-9

What practices or ideology do our Christian culture (and sometimes our churches) try to "teach as doctrine" that are actually man made ideas?

The religious leaders may have meant well. They may have started young and bright-eyed with hearts surrendered to God. But, somewhere along the way, they lost sight of the goal. And when it really counted, they couldn't see the truth standing right in front of them.

Like it or not, we can easily behave like these religious leaders. I wish I could shake the religious leaders in this story and say, "*What are you doing? Go WITH the Wise Men! This is what you've all been waiting for!*"

What areas in your life are you stubborn about? Unmovable in your vision? What if you opened your heart a bit to the idea that you might be wrong?

If there's an area in your life that you've held onto for a long time, convinced of your innocence or rightness, I would encourage you to humble yourself and present this area to God with fresh eyes and a willingness to reevaluate your heart in the matter.

Ask God to forgive you for the times, because of stubbornness or pride, you were unable to see Him right in front of you.

December

21

Read Matthew 2:9-12
Write Matthew 2:10

What stands out to you in these verses and why?

The Wise Men had a hunch about the star. They were 97% sure this star would lead them somewhere. And then, they find what they're looking for. And they erupt with joy.

I love the star and its beautiful parallels to what God does in our lives. The star goes before us. Sometimes you don't even realize what you're seeking, until its found.

What did the Wise Men do when they entered the house of Jesus?

What do you imagine were the emotions felt by Mary and Joseph at this encounter?

What is more significant than the posture they assume in Jesus' presence or the generous gifts they presented, is the beauty of whom was presenting them. God had wielded the cosmos so that Jesus was worshiped that night, not by devout Jews—those who most anxiously awaited his arrival—but, by men from the east. Gentiles.

The significance of the Wise Men in this story is that they point to God's great plan. That all nations would worship Jesus. The Messiah has not only come to save Jews, but every nation, tribe and tongue.

LOVE COMES NEAR

Read Exodus 13:21, Psalm 139:5-12, Isaiah 45:2

Throughout the Bible, you will read about God going before his people. Especially when the Jews were wandering in the wilderness. The word "wandering" seems so aimless, and they were at it for 40 years. I think it's easy to imagine that it *was* aimless. But, there was purpose in their wandering. There was a necessary work that God was doing in the Israelite people during this time. And it wasn't aimless. Exodus 13:21 tells us that he went before them day and night.

The NLT version of Psalm 139:5 says, "*You go before me and follow me. You place your hand of blessing on my head.*"

What a beautiful promise. He goes before me, graciously making a way. He follows behind me, like a protective father.

The Wise Men had done their homework. They had studied the stars, they charted their course, they knew the prophecies. They were ready for the adventure when it was presented. And the payoff? *Great joy.*

What dream in your heart are you neglecting? What course in life is God calling you to chart? What homework needs your attention?

How does the promise in Psalms inspire your courage for adventure? What lesson do you learn from the star in the Christmas story?

This Christmas, watch for the star. When you see a star as you're shopping, when you admire the star on top of your Christmas tree, let it lead you to this promise: God goes before us. There is no aimless wandering, no accidents, when you are a child of the King.

Read Matthew 2:13-15
Write Hosea 11:1

Of all the places that the angel could have sent them, Egypt is the safest? Egypt, with its painful memories of Israelite torment, is the place God has chosen as a refuge for his son. I like how Matthew Henry's Commentary explained it: "God, when he pleases, can make the worst of places serve the best of purposes."

What images or experiences does that statement bring to mind?

Without hesitation, Joseph awakens Mary in the night and flees immediately with Jesus. They have likely been in Bethlehem for about two years; a young couple, trying to build a life and make a living, when God says, "Go!"

Would you have the faith to go without hesitation as Joseph did? Have you ever witnessed (or been called to) this kind of faith in your life?

Again, Matthew connects the old and the new, in this passage and in the few to follow. He shows how Jesus life repeats certain aspects of Israel's history. Matthew points to Jesus fulfillment of the prophecy stated in Hosea 11:1. These words in Hosea were originally spoken about Israel named as God's chosen people and now point to Jesus, God's *true* son.

LOVE COMES NEAR

In our culture, and in our wealth, we can often miss the opportunity for complete reliance on God to meet our needs. Money serves as the god of choice for many. Even for believers, who don't stand guard against temptation.

Relocating to a new city, or a new country, is no small task. When the angel woke up Joseph in the night, he didn't give them time to prepare. Which is why the timing of the Wise Men's gift is so precise and so precious in this story.

This gift was providential and likely helped them get established in their new home. God comes near us in the details of our life. He meets our every need.

How have you seen God provide for you in unexpected ways? Have you ever been in a position of great need, or witnessed a great need, where God stepped in?

Read Matthew 6:25-34 and Philippians 4:19

Are you guilty of worrying about your needs being met? How can you begin to lay your worries down and "*seek first the kingdom?*"

Read Matthew 2:16-18
Write Job 5:12-13

Herod thinks he's outsmarted God. He wields his earthly power, but it's no match for His.

Reflect on the verses you wrote today from Job. What emotions do you feel reading these verses?

How do you reconcile the horrific massacre of innocent life, with the knowledge that God's sovereignty stands?

The prophecy spoken by Jeremiah, originally personified Rachel as representative of all the mother's in Israel. When the prophet first spoke these words, they pointed to the Israelites being exiled from their home. And because Israel was no longer a nation, it was as though they are dead. But, now, in the Christmas story, we see the prophecy further fulfilled as a mother's worst nightmare comes true, when her innocent child is murdered.

LOVE COMES NEAR

How is there anything good or comforting to draw from this tragedy in the Christmas story? I'm not sure there is.

But, we can certainly use it as a reminder of our own loss and the loss of others. Christmas is a time of great celebration, but for many — perhaps even for you — it can be an especially difficult time of year.

The Bible says that God has set eternity in our hearts. **Read Ecclesiastes 3:11.**

We were created with a longing for home. And a knowledge that this isn't it. I believe that on earth we experience that same longing for home in our families. And it's why there can be so much pain associated with this season. Whether it's loss through death or broken relationships, Christmas with all its talk of family and memories and meals around the table, can invoke a lot of pain for some.

If you are suffering because of a loss this Christmas, I pray that you feel wrapped up in His promise of comfort. **Read Psalm 34:18.**

If you have not experienced a significant loss, I'm sure you know of someone who has or who is hurting because of broken relationships. **Ask God how he might lead you to reach out to them this Christmas.**

We may not hold any earthly answers to the pain of our loss, but we do hold an eternal hope. And by showing love to others in their loss, we can be a reminder of that hope, as we wait for His return.

Read Matthew 2:19-23
Write John 1:46

Expect the unexpected when it comes to God's story. The entire telling of Jesus' birth has been marked by radical humility. The Savior of the world comes to us as a baby, born in a stable. His humble beginning is followed now by a humble upbringing, in a town despised by men.

John 1:46 is spoken by a skeptical Nathanael, after his friend Philip told him they had found the one "*Moses wrote about in the Law, and about whom the prophets also wrote...*" (John 1:45)

Nazareth was small and insignificant. There's no way anything worthwhile could come out of that place. *Everybody knows that.*

Jesus example of humility is for us to follow. Radical humility. Humbling ourselves in a way that the world takes notice. Humbling ourselves in a way that leaves no room for personal praise, but only a reason to give God praise.

What is your greatest testament to a life of humility? How have you seen God work through humble circumstances?

How can you practically seek to humble yourself in a world that screams of self praise and promotion?

LOVE COMES NEAR

Fill in the blank: I could never _____.

Impossible circumstances, inadequate education, insurmountable odds. There's no excuse or justification too difficult for God. Overcoming the impossible is His sweet spot.

How are the odds stacked against you in the pursuit of your dreams? List them out, then say a prayer and acknowledge that these obstacles are no match for God.

Remember the angel's words to Mary? **Read Luke 1:37**

He can bring forth life from a virgin and open a barren womb. He can lead Wise Men with a star in the sky and direct the decisions of kings. He can cause an explosion of celebration in the sky and make the greatest of the least.

Nothing is impossible with God. *Not one thing.*

Christmas DAY

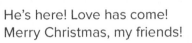

He's here! Love has come!
Merry Christmas, my friends!

Advent Family Calendar

This simple Advent Family Calendar will allow you to share Christmas story reflections with your kids, grandkids, or any special kids in your life. Use the chart and mark each day or use the cut-outs to include in your family's Advent calendar.

Each day, you're given one passage to read, one verse to write and a question or thought to consider. The questions were written with kids, ages 6-12, in mind. But, I would encourage you to make any modifications you think appropriate, based on the ages and stages of your own family.

You can enjoy this simple activity during mealtimes or at bedtime. Whatever works for you. Any version of the scriptures you prefer is great, but I really like the NIRV (New International Readers Version) when I'm looking at scripture with my kids. You can access it online or from your YouVersion Bible App.

☐ DECEMBER 1
Read Exodus 24:1-2; Write Hebrews 4:16
How would it feel if we couldn't talk directly to God? What does it mean to approach God's throne with confidence?

☐ DECEMBER 2
Read Isaiah 9:2-7; Write Isaiah 9:6
Look at all the names of Jesus you wrote from Isaiah 9:6. Which one is your favorite? Why?

☐ DECEMBER 3
Read Isaiah 11:1-5, 10; Write Isaiah 11:2
Draw a picture of a tiny branch growing out from an old dead tree stump. Display your picture and think about how the new branch represents Jesus and his gift of eternal hope and joy, whenever you see it.

☐ DECEMBER 4
Read Jeremiah 33:14-16
Write Jeremiah 33:16
This passage also talks about the new branch and reminds us that God is a promise keeper. Have you ever not been sure that someone would keep their promise? Why is keeping promises so important?

☐ DECEMBER 5
Read Hebrews 7:18-19
Write Hebrews 7:18-19
Why do you think it can sometimes be hard to follow the rules? Jesus came so all of us (even the kids who don't always follow the rules) can have a chance to know Him and be near Him. It's just one of God's many Christmas gifts to us, through Jesus.

☐ DECEMBER 6
Read Matthew 1:1-16; Write John 15:16
All of these names are people who weren't perfect, but who God chose anyway to be a part of his story. How does it make you feel to know that God chose you to be in his story, too?

☐ DECEMBER 7
Read Luke 1:5-17; Write Luke 1:13
Zechariah and Elizabeth loved God, even when they didn't get their way. But, after a long wait, God blesses them by answering their prayer for a baby. Do you ever feel like God doesn't hear your prayers? What do you learn from Zechariah and Elizabeth's story?

Read Luke 1:18-25; Write John 1:16
Zechariah made a mistake by not believing the message from God at first. But, God gives us his grace for our mistakes. Grace is like a band-aid; he covers our mistakes and give us a new chance. He still blessed Zechariah and he can still bless us, even when we mess up. Talk about what it means to you to have God's grace.

Read Luke 1:26-38; Write Luke 1:37
Imagine if you were Mary. How would you feel if an angel showed up at your house? The angel gives Mary a big job and she says, "Yes!" What's the hardest challenge in your life right now? God wants to teach us that even when things feel difficult, there's nothing too hard for Him.

Read Luke 1:39-45; Write Luke 1:45
When something amazing happens in your life, who usually gets the credit? Mary and Elizabeth were chosen by God to do big things and their first response is to give praise to God. Even the baby in Elizabeth's belly praised God. Every blessing we have in life is from God. Will you be first to give God praise?

Read Luke 1:46-56
Write Luke 1:49
This passage is called "Mary's Song," and it's full of thankfulness and praise. Write down two things that you are thankful for today and two ways that God has blessed your life.

Read Matthew 1:18-21
Write Matthew 1:21
Joseph is faced with a tough decision, but he chooses to believe God, even though it doesn't make sense at first. Faith means we believe it, even when we can't always see it. Like when you sit on a chair, you trust (or have faith) that it will hold you. Every time we believe God, our faith grows. Why does God want our faith to grow?

Read Matthew 1:22-24
Write Matthew 1:23
Jesus is called many different names in the Bible. At Christmas time we hear and sing about Jesus' name, Immanuel. What does this passage tell us "Immanuel" means? What does it mean that God is "with us?"

Read Micah 5:2-5a; Write Micah 5:5a
This is another Old Testament passage that has clues in it about Jesus. There's an adventure inside the Bible, if we're willing to take the journey. God's word fits together like a puzzle, with no missing pieces and no mistakes. Why is it important that God's words are 100% true?

Read Luke 2:1-7; Write Luke 2:7
God makes it possible for Mary and Joseph to get safely to Bethlehem, but he doesn't see to it that they have a room to stay in. Why do you think God would want his son to be born in a stable? Why do we have challenging times, even though God is big enough to make them simple?

Read Luke 2:8-12; Write Luke 2:10
The angels appear many times in the Christmas story, and their message from God always begins with, "*Do not fear...*" God doesn't want us to be afraid. We can trust His promise, that he is always with us. This Christmas season, every time you see an angel, let it remind you that you have nothing to fear, because God is with you.

Read Luke 2:13-18; Write Luke 2:14
When the angels appear to the shepherds, they don't hesitate to go and announce it to their town. We should always be bold in sharing about Jesus, too. When God does something good in your life, how can you share about it with your family and friends?

Read Luke 2:19-21; Write Luke 2:19
Mary has been through so much in a short time. She doesn't want to forget a thing, so she spends time thinking about them, to lock them in her memory. What do you do when you want to remember something? We should take time to do this with the things we learn about God, too.

Read Matthew 2:1-2; Write Isaiah 60:3
The Wise Men saw the great light and they followed it. Today, we still follow the light of Jesus. Talk about how Jesus is like a light in the dark.

Read Matthew 2:3-8; Write Matthew 15:8
Herod was an evil king. Do you think he meant it when he said he wanted to worship Jesus? God wants us to be sincere in our love for him. Talk about why God wants our hearts and not just our words and actions to honor him.

Read Matthew 2:9-12
Write Matthew 2:10
The Wise Men were very wise men. They had a talent for studying the stars. They had studied a long time and so when this star appeared, they knew it was special. God has given each of us interests and talents. He wants us to practice and use them so that we can be ready to do the work he has planned for us. What are the interests and talents you can work on and use for God?

Read Matthew 2:13-15
Write Philippians 4:19
Joseph heard from the angel again, and was again told to "Go!" Joseph has no time to prepare. He gets Mary and baby Jesus up in the night to flee to Egypt. Talk about God's promises to meet our needs, even when we can't see how he will do it.

Read Matthew 2:16-18; Write Psalm 34:18
This is a sad, but true, story. Because there is sin in our world, bad things happen. We may never understand why, but we can trust that God is still in charge and he promises to comfort us. What are some different ways that God comforts us when we are sad?

Read Matthew 2:19-23
Write 1 Samuel 16:7
Have you heard the expression, "Don't judge a book by its cover?" Sometimes we make a decision about something or someone, before we really know the truth about it. It's what humans do. But, God looks at our heart first. Nazareth was not a great place to live and many people thought that nothing good could ever come from there. But, God wants us to know that he can use anything, any place or any person to accomplish his plan.

Read and write John 1:14
It's Christmas day, and Jesus is here! Don't forget the true reason we celebrate and the gift that God gave us when he sent his son. Merry Christmas!

December 1

Read Exodus 24:1-2
Write Hebrews 4:16

December 2

Read Isaiah 9:2-7
Write Isaiah 9:6

December 3

Read Isaiah 11:1-5, 10
Write Isaiah 11:2

December 4

Read Jeremiah 33:14-16
Write Jeremiah 33:16

How would it feel if we couldn't talk directly to God? What does it mean to approach God's throne with confidence?

Look at all the names of Jesus you wrote from Isaiah 9:6. Which one is your favorite? Why?

Draw a picture of a tiny branch growing out from an old dead tree stump. Display your picture and think about how the new branch represents Jesus and his gift of eternal hope and joy, whenever you see it.

This passage also talks about the new branch and reminds us that God is a promise keeper. Have you ever not been sure that someone would keep their promise? Why is keeping promises so important?

December
5

Read Hebrews 7:18-19
Write Hebrews 7:18-19

December
6

Read Matthew 1:1-16
Write John 15:16

December
7

Read Luke 1:5-17
Write Luke 1:13

December
8

Read Luke 1:18-25
Write John 1:16

Why do you think it can sometimes be hard to follow the rules? Jesus came so all of us (even the kids who don't always follow the rules) can have a chance to know Him and be near Him. It's just one of God's many Christmas gifts to us, through Jesus.

- -

All of these names are people who weren't perfect, but who God chose anyway to be a part of his story. How does it make you feel to know that God chose you to be in his story, too?

- -

Zechariah and Elizabeth loved God, even when they didn't get their way. But, after a long wait, God blesses them by answering their prayer for a baby. Do you ever feel like God doesn't hear your prayers? What do you learn from Zechariah and Elizabeth's story?

- -

Zechariah made a mistake by not believing the message from God at first. But, God gives us his grace for our mistakes. Grace is like a band-aid; he covers our mistakes and give us a new chance. He still blessed Zechariah and he can still bless us, even when we mess up. Talk about what it means to you to have God's grace.

December
9

Read Luke 1:26-38
Write Luke 1:37

December
10

Read Luke 1:39-45
Write Luke 1:45

December
11

Read Luke 1:46-56
Write Luke 1:49

December
12

Read Matthew 1:18-21
Write Matthew 1:21

Imagine if you were Mary. How would you feel if an angel showed up at your house? The angel gives Mary a big job and she says, "Yes!" What's the hardest challenge in your life right now? God wants to teach us that even when things feel difficult, there's nothing too hard for Him.

When something amazing happens in your life, who usually gets the credit? Mary and Elizabeth were chosen by God to do big things and their first response is to give praise to God. Even the baby in Elizabeth's belly praised God. Every blessing we have in life is from God. Will you be first to give God praise?

This passage is called "Mary's Song," and it's full of thankfulness and praise. Write down two things that you are thankful for today and two ways that God has blessed your life.

Joseph is faced with a tough decision, but he chooses to believe God, even though it doesn't make sense at first. Faith means we believe it, even when we can't always see it. Like when you sit on a chair, you trust (or have faith) that it will hold you. Every time we believe God, our faith grows. Why does God want our faith to grow?

 Read Matthew 1:22-24
Write Matthew 1:23

 Read Micah 5:2-5a
Write Micah 5:5a

 Read Luke 2:1-7
Write Luke 2:7

 Read Luke 2:8-12
Write Luke 2:10

Jesus is called many different names in the Bible. At Christmas time we hear and sing about Jesus' name, Immanuel. What does this passage tell us "Immanuel" means? What does it mean that God is "with us?"

- -

This is another Old Testament passage that has clues in it about Jesus. There's an adventure inside the Bible, if we're willing to take the journey. God's word fits together like a puzzle, with no missing pieces and no mistakes. Why is it important that God's words are 100% true?

- -

God makes it possible for Mary and Joseph to get safely to Bethlehem, but he doesn't see to it that they have a room to stay in. Why do you think God would want his son to be born in a stable? Why do we have challenging times, even though God is big enough to make them simple?

- -

The angels appear many times in the Christmas story, and their message from God always begins with, "*Do not fear...*" God doesn't want us to be afraid. We can trust His promise, that he is always with us. This Christmas season, every time you see an angel, let it remind you that you have nothing to fear, because God is with you.

Read Luke 2:13-18
Write Luke 2:14

Read Luke 2:19-21
Write Luke 2:19

Read Matthew 2:1-2
Write Isaiah 60:3

Read Matthew 2:3-8
Write Matthew 15:8

When the angels appear to the shepherds, they don't hesitate to go and announce it to their town. We should always be bold in sharing about Jesus, too. When God does something good in your life, how can you share about it with your family and friends?

Mary has been through so much in a short time. She doesn't want to forget a thing, so she spends time thinking about them, to lock them in her memory. What do you do when you want to remember something? We should take time to do this with the things we learn about God, too.

The Wise Men saw the great light and they followed it. Today, we still follow the light of Jesus. Talk about how Jesus is like a light in the dark.

Herod was an evil king. Do you think he meant it when he said he wanted to worship Jesus? God wants us to be sincere in our love for him. Talk about why God wants our hearts and not just our words and actions to honor him.

December
21

Read Matthew 2:9-12
Write Matthew 2:10

December
22

Read Matthew 2:13-15
Write Philippians 4:19

December
23

Read Matthew 2:16-18
Write Psalm 34:18

December
24

Read Matthew 2:19-23
Write 1 Samuel 16:7

December
25

Read and write John 1:14

The Wise Men were very wise men. They had a talent for studying the stars. They had studied a long time and so when this star appeared, they knew it was special. God has given each of us interests and talents. He wants us to practice and use them so that we can be ready to do the work he has planned for us. What are the interests and talents you can work on and use for God?

Joseph heard from the angel again, and was again told to "Go!" Joseph has no time to prepare. He gets Mary and baby Jesus up in the night to flee to Egypt. Talk about God's promises to meet our needs, even when we can't see how he will do it.

This is a sad, but true, story. Because there is sin in our world, bad things happen. We may never understand why, but we can trust that God is still in charge and he promises to comfort us. What are some different ways that God comforts us when we are sad?

Have you heard the expression, "Don't judge a book by its cover?" Sometimes we make a decision about something or someone, before we really know the truth about it. It's what humans do. But, God looks at our heart first. Nazareth was not a great place to live and many people thought that nothing good could ever come from there. But, God wants us to know that he can use anything, any place or any person to accomplish his plan.

It's Christmas day, and Jesus is here! Don't forget the true reason we celebrate and the gift that God gave us when he sent his son. Merry Christmas!

Made in the USA
Monee, IL
31 October 2019